Sunny Hills Elementary
3200 Issaquah Pine Lk. Rd.
Sammamish, WA 98075

Richard Peck

The Library of Author Biographies™

RICHARD PECK

Michael A. Sommers

The Rosen Publishing Group, Inc., New York

To Oscar and Vladimir Sommers-Campbell

Published in 2004 by The Rosen Publishing Group, Inc.
29 East 21st Street, New York, NY 10010

Library of Congress Cataloging-in-Publication Data

Sommers, Michael A., 1966–
Richard Peck / Michael A. Sommers.
    p. cm. — (The library of author biographies)
Includes bibliographical references and index.
ISBN 0-8239-4018-7 (lib. bdg.)
1. Peck, Richard, 1934– 2. Novelists, American—20th century—Biography. 3. Young adult fiction—Authorship.
I. Title. II. Series.
PS3566.E2526Z88 2003
818'.5409—dc21

2002155677

Manufactured in the United States of America

Excerpt from *Presenting Richard Peck*, by Donald R. Gallo, Twayne Publishers, © 1989, Twayne Publishers. Reprinted by permission of the Gale Group.
Interview with Richard Peck copyright © 2003 by Richard Peck. All rights reserved. Used with permission.

Table of Contents

Introduction:
A Paradox
Named Peck

Richard Peck is one of the most widely read and critically acclaimed authors of young adult fiction in North America. In a career that spans more than thirty years, he has published thirty novels for young people. He has also written countless essays and articles, a handful of poems, four adult novels, and a picture book for children. Furthermore, Richard Peck is a paradox.

A paradox is someone or something that has qualities or ideas that, on the surface, seem to contradict or conflict with each other. For example, Richard Peck was so fed up with teaching junior high school English

that, at the age of thirty-seven, he left the classroom for good in order to write young adult
novels. Today, however, not only does he still
consider himself a teacher, he also travels thousands of miles a year visiting schools and
talking to students. And this is only one of
Peck's many paradoxes.

If you have read any of Peck's interviews
or autobiographical books, you might find his
passion for teens surprising. This is because Peck
has never been shy about criticizing youth in
general. As a group, Peck finds the young people
of today to be unmotivated, rootless, conformist,
consumer-crazed, brand-conscious, computer-
addicted, uninformed . . . and that's just a start.
And yet, few other young adult and children's
authors spend as much time talking to and
researching young people, let alone actually
hanging out with them. Peck estimates that he
spends a quarter of his professional life as a writer
in schools and libraries with kids, and he wouldn't
have it any other way. In a 1985 essay published in
The Horn Book Magazine, Peck summed up why
staying in close contact with kids is so important
to him:

> Content with small gains and minor break-
> throughs, we writers and teachers and librarians

turn to the young because they can still astonish us. We're qualified idealists [dreamers who believe in a better world]—who believe that a printed page can breathe, and we'd like to share that news with newcomers.[1]

Although he has lived most of his adult life in New York City, the majority of his novels take place in new suburbs or small Midwestern towns. And while his novels are for and about young people and their problems, some of his best-loved and most memorable characters are elderly people. Though he has written two novels about cyberspace, Peck is so wary of technology that he still types all his novels on an electric typewriter. Also ironic is the fact that though he hates shopping malls, he has penned two highly successful books that are satires about malls.

Peck is great at finding out what his readers want and then giving it to them—but always with an unexpected twist. For example, when his readers' letters clamored for a romance, he wrote a novel called *Close Enough to Touch* (1981). It was about a boy and a girl in love, the girl dying, and the boy coming to terms with loneliness. And when his readers wanted ghost stories and science fiction, he came up with a series of books whose time-traveling heroine, Blossom Culp, was the class misfit who had to deal with timeless problems of cliques and peer pressure.

Critics have praised Peck for capturing the speech patterns, slang, and fashions of teendom like few other young adult (YA) authors. At the same time, a surprising number of his novels take place in the past and are full of historical figures and details that are unknown to most of his young readers. Furthermore, while his books tackle serious issues such as death and divorce, poverty and pregnancy, rape and romance, they are also highly entertaining and often very humorous.

Nonetheless, although his young protagonists are always stronger and wiser by the novel's end, it is a rare Peck book that ends happily with all problems neatly solved. Ultimately, while Peck takes great pains to find out what his readers want, he also loves nothing more than to challenge their expectations. As he has often been quoted saying:

> I believe I have one theme in all of my books and I want to get it across to all my readers every time, and that is this: You will never begin to grow up until you declare your independence from your peers.[2]

1 Storytelling

There are people who seem to have been born writing. There are others who come to writing later in life. I fall into this latter category, never having written a line of fiction until I was thirty-seven years old. But I was born listening— eavesdropping, if you like.[1]

Richard Wayne Peck was born on April 5, 1934, in Decatur, Illinois. A midsized Midwest town, Decatur was full of history. Dennis Avenue, where Richard lived until the age of eighteen, was paved with bricks and lined with colonial Dutch houses. Across the street from the Peck house, sprawling Fairview Park boasted ancient oak trees and the town's first public building—an 1829 log courthouse where young Abraham Lincoln worked as a judge.

Richard's father, Wayne Morris Peck, grew up on a farm and had wonderful memories of a childhood that included fishing, hunting, and diving into swimming holes. In the seventh grade, he dropped out of school and hopped freight trains to the Dakotas where he earned his keep harvesting wheat. When World War I broke out, Wayne went to fight with American forces in France. He returned home partially disabled from a shattered left shoulder, and he found that life had changed. The "good old days" of his youth were no more.

Wayne Peck often relived his golden boyhood in the tales he told his son. Listening to his father recount his memories, young Richard had the sensation that he had been "born after the party was over."[2] He also learned about "nostalgia as an art form."[3] This longing for the past would stay with Richard Peck throughout his life and influence many of his novels.

Unable to do heavy farmwork, Wayne opened a gas station on the "other"—poorer—side of town. Unlike the other fathers Richard knew, who went to work in ironed shirts and jackets, his father thundered off to work in overalls on a

Harley Davidson motorcycle. He ran his gas station like a private club where truckers and farmers hung around swapping stories polished "with years of retelling and flavored . . . with tobacco juice."[4]

Richard's father and his world weren't the only sources of stories in the young boy's life. His mother, Virginia Gray, was the middle child of seven siblings who came from a well-off Illinois farming family. As a child, Richard spent time at his grandparents' Walnut Grove Farm with its long porches, massive trees, and endless lawns. Here he was surrounded by a group of elderly women: his grandmother, Flossie Mae Gray, and her four sisters, Lura, Maude, Pearl, and Ozena. Whenever the family got together, Richard would hang around the kitchen and listen to them recount tales from the past.

Another great source of stories was Richard's much-loved and eccentric great uncle Miles. Says Peck, "He worked when he wanted to; he fished when he wanted to; and he said rude things in front of people's mothers. I thought he was God."[5] Growing up amid so many interesting adults, so much history, and so many stories had a great impact on Richard Peck. These voices remained in his memory and, years later, inspired many of the characters, events, and patterns of speech in his fiction. As Peck says, "When you write to young readers, you need the wisdom of those people at the other end of life. I came to writing with an entire crew of seasoned elders on my side."[6]

Home Life

At home, Richard Peck's mother, Virginia, a professional dietician, was frequently inventing new recipes. She was helped by her husband, who would often go fishing and hunting for freshwater fish and exotic game, which he would then clean and prepare. Together, the two of them would make fantastic meals, and there was always company on hand to help sample their inventive dishes.

During World War II (1939–1945), when Richard was a young boy, meat and other food supplies were often rationed. However, between Wayne's hunting and the chickens, pigs, and calves sent down from Walnut Grove Farm, the Pecks were never short of food. There was often even enough to share with the neighbors. In fact, the neighborhood kids with strong stomachs always came running whenever word went around that Wayne Peck was preparing to wring the necks of two chickens: one to freeze, the other to fry. Richard's memories of breaking chickens' necks made it into one of his earliest novels, *Representing Super Doll* (1974):

> Mama has her own way of killing . . . [She] plants her feet apart right in the middle of the yard and screws up her face like it's going to hurt her worse than the victim. Then she begins to swing the bird in big cartwheels at an angle over her head.
>
> Mama's not a big woman, and along with Dad she's as gentle a human being as ever lived. But that first swing is a neckbreaker, which is a mercy for the chicken. She keeps whipping it around and around though, until the body parts company with the head and goes jumping and spreading feathers all over the yard.[7]

According to Peck, this opening to his fourth novel made his New York City publishers and suburban readers quite squeamish. However, for Peck the scene was not only a tip of the hat to his father, but a "useful antidote [remedy] [for] a world steadily being engulfed by Chicken McNuggets."[8]

Before Richard could read by himself, his mother read to him. Early favorites included Grimm's fairy tales (such as "Hansel and Gretel"), Aesop's fables, (such as "The Ant and the Grasshopper"), and the adventure tales of Robert

Louis Stevenson (such as *Treasure Island*, 1883). He particularly liked the real-life adventures of an American explorer named Richard Halliburton. An Indiana Jones-like character, Halliburton led his readers to far-flung destinations and introduced them to foreign cultures ranging from the Mayan to the Mediterranean. Young Richard was seduced by these accounts of other realities that beckoned from beyond the safe world of Decatur.

As an adult, Richard Peck has said that his mother reading to him at an early age before he began school was what awakened his desire to be a writer. Listening to the radio was another early influence. During Richard's childhood, radio as a vehicle of information and entertainment was as important as television is today. In a recent interview, Peck describes how "radio used words to create characters, to weave plots, and to invite the imagination, and I think that probably made a novelist out of me."[9] Lying on the floor in front of his family's Philco radio, young Richard dreamed of being a writer. He also dreamed of traveling to London and of living in New York.

Future Plans

Richard marched into his first day of kindergarten on the same day that Hitler's Nazi forces marched into Poland, on September 1, 1939. His private kindergarten classes were held in a big old house belonging to the teacher, Miss Howe. In the middle of each morning, Miss Beth Butts would play piano and the kids would march around the room. When it was young Richard's turn to suggest a marching song, he requested "Sidewalks of New York." He recalls:

> "Why do you want that song?" Miss Butts inquired.
> "Because I'll be moving to New York."
> "Really?" She knew my parents well and how firmly rooted they were. "Soon?"
> "Well, as soon as I can get there," I said.[10]

2 School Days

orld War II was in full swing when
Richard Peck began grade school.
Despite food rationing, some aspects of war proved exciting. At school, posters warned students against the dangers of discussing military secrets because "Loose Lips Sink Ships." With their copycat military haircuts, Richard and his friends formed air force squadrons. During recess they zoomed across the schoolyard, their arms stretched out like airplane wings as they pretended to bomb Berlin.

In the classrooms, maps were decorated with multicolored pushpins representing "Our Troops" and "Their Troops." In this wartime atmosphere, teachers laid down rules with military precision and students obediently followed them. Arriving late for school, not completing a homework assignment, even

18

making a spelling mistake was somehow seen as unpatriotic.

At school, both teachers and students were gung ho about U.S. participation in the war. At home, however, Wayne Peck was critical of America's role in the war. After all, Richard's father had fought and been wounded in "the War to end all wars," World War I. The fact that America's young men were once again sacrificing their lives a generation later left him feeling depressed.

This difference in opinion between adults at school and at home left an impression on Richard. As he later remarked: "Nothing interests a child more than adults disagreeing . . . I awoke to the interesting point that adults don't provide a united front. This alerted me to viewpoint, which is a novelist's stock in trade. Writers aren't nearly as interested in what happens as in their characters' various and conflicting points of view."[1]

The Fox-Trot and the Big Apple

When he was in third grade, Richard's younger sister, Cheryl, was born. Richard admits that during their childhood he was the older brother who followed the rules while Cheryl was the younger sibling who broke them. At Woodrow Wilson Junior High School, Richard, like all students, obeyed and respected his teachers. "I did my homework out of fear, not goodness," he confessed to his biographer, Donald Gallo. "From junior high on, I thought that the only safe way to a scholarship was a string of A's on the report card."[2]

When not at school or doing homework, Richard had other responsibilities. One was the daily after-school paper route he shared with his best friend, Chick Wolfe. Another was Miss Van Dyke's dance class, where every other week, Decatur's boys and girls got dressed up and learned how to waltz, fox-trot, and rumba across the floor. Those who couldn't "cut a rug" (or dance) by high school were considered social misfits by their peers. In high school, Richard continued to study hard and he dreamed of becoming a writer. Three of the most important subjects he studied were history, Latin, and geography. They proved to be handy tools for a future novelist, providing him with "something to say, how to say it, and somewhere to set the story."[3]

The summer he was sixteen, Richard's dreams of going to New York City became a reality when he was invited to visit a distant relative. Arriving in the Big Apple, he was very relieved to discover that "the outside world was really there and somewhat better than the movies." As he said, "It occurred to me that this was the place I'd been homesick for all along."[4]

"Miss F"

Back in Decatur for his final year of high school, Richard studied hard, hoping to win a college scholarship. However, one obstacle loomed on the horizon: Miss Franklin, the senior English teacher. All students feared her and, unfortunately, there was no avoiding her. On the first day of school, she made a fierce announcement to the class: "I can get all of you in this room into the colleges of your choices . . . or I can keep you out."[5] Richard, who had always been a straight-A student, was somewhat shocked when the first composition he wrote for "Miss F" was returned without a grade. Instead, Miss Franklin had written on the paper: "Never express yourself again on my time. Find a more interesting topic."[6]

As Peck recalls in his autobiography, *Anonymously Yours* (1991):

> Well, I was seventeen. I didn't know what a more interesting topic than me would be. I actually went to the woman and asked, "What would a more interesting topic be?"
> "Almost anything," she replied.
> That led me to the library, a place I'd been successfully avoiding up until then, in search of subject matter that was not me.[7]

In his English class, Peck didn't write fiction, but he did learn the importance of communication. And much more emphasis was placed on grammar than on imagination. After all, how could you set down your wildest ideas if you couldn't string a sentence together? From Miss F, Richard Peck learned that real writing is rewriting. Which is why to this day Peck rewrites each page of a novel at least six times. Miss F also taught him that writing wasn't about expressing yourself, but about communicating with readers. It is a lesson that has guided Peck ever since. As an adult novelist writing for adolescents, he is constantly asking himself who his readers are and how to reach them through words.

Off to England

In the spring of 1952, several important things happened in Richard's life. He won a scholarship to DePauw University in Greencastle, Indiana; he graduated from high school; he celebrated his eighteenth birthday, and, as an American male "adult," he had to register for required military service at his local draft board. Like all young men going to college, Richard was allowed to defer his two-year service until graduation, providing he maintained a high grade-point average.

Peck entered college, still with the secret dream of being a writer. Unfortunately, in the Midwest, nobody, including Richard himself, considered "novelist" to be a stable profession that would pay the bills. A more practical career choice, one that would earn him a good income while keeping him close to the written word, was that of English teacher.

One advantage to studying English at DePauw was that students in their junior year could spend a year at Exeter University in southwest England. Having been to New York, Peck jumped at the chance of making his dream to visit England come true. Exeter is an attractive medieval city set amid rolling green hills. Although he found the food—lots of mashed potatoes and brussels sprouts— rather dull, Richard got along very well with his fellow students and professors. His two best friends were worldly, brilliant students with fascinating life stories. And his professors opened his eyes in various ways.

Peck returned to America wearing heavy English tweed jackets and with a toned-down Midwestern accent. He finished his final year at DePauw and graduated. He was now ready and qualified to teach English. Instead, however, he was snatched up by the U.S. Army and sent to fulfill his two-year military service in West Germany.

3 Traveling

When he first went off to West Germany, Peck expected the worst. He had visions of two years in a muddy trench, glaring through barbed wire at the rifle of an East German soldier. Instead, he found himself based in a pretty German town called Ansbach, where he discovered two important things about being in the army during peacetime. First, there was a great deal of paperwork to be dealt with. Secondly, there were few people around who could read or write well enough to deal with it. Because of this, Peck—who could type—became quite valued. He began his army stint by writing up daily reports. Although the job came with the benefits of having a warm stove to sit beside and plenty of opportunities to read books, Peck soon grew restless.

One Sunday, while sitting in the chapel, Peck realized that the soldiers around him were bored by the chaplain's sermon. That same afternoon, Peck whipped up a sermon that discussed issues relevant to lonely soldiers far from home. He slipped it under the chaplain's door and was pleased to hear the chaplain reading it aloud the following Sunday. Peck was careful to be caught when, the following week, he slid another sermon beneath the chaplain's door. This way, he was able to meet the chaplain. The chaplain was impressed with the young soldier's writing style. He was being transferred to the city of Stuttgart, and he asked Peck, who had grown up attending church, if he would like to come along as his assistant.

As a chaplain's assistant, Peck found himself not only writing weekly sermons, but conducting the chaplain's marriage counseling sessions as well. At night, while he was writing, soldiers often came to visit him, seeking chaplain's advice for personal problems. The experience brought Peck one step closer to becoming a good novelist. He polished his writing skills and got used to working under a deadline. He also learned that much of being a good writer comes from being a good listener.

Journeys

Whenever he had leave, Peck took the opportunity to travel around Europe. Travel not only continued to open up new worlds for Peck, but also showed him the value of being on his own and fending for himself in a foreign place. As he later said, "Anyone just about to leave adolescence needs to cut himself out of the pack and be on his own."[1]

One of his favorite cities was London, which he never tired of exploring. In fact, it later provided the setting for his third novel, *Through a Brief Darkness* (1973). In the novel, sixteen-year-old Karen Beatty, the unsuspecting daughter of a New York gangster, is kidnapped and flown to London by her father's enemies. Plunged into a dangerous situation, Karen must use her wits in order to survive and escape. Her experiences in England force her to think and act in ways she never would have had to at home.

Many of the teenage protagonists in Peck's novels become older and wiser by taking trips and chances away from home. Whether traveling from the safety of a small town to a big city, such as

Carol in *Don't Look and It Won't Hurt* (1972), or from the supposed sophistication of a big city in comparison to a small town, such as what Joey and his sister Mary Alice experience in the Newbery Award-winning *A Long Way from Chicago* (1998), and its sequel, *A Year Down Yonder* (2000), these trips are important because they remove characters from the safety of home and their usual groups of friends. Travel is the means by which Peck's characters discover their own individual identities. It also helps them define key relationships with close friends and family members.

In *Those Summer Girls I Never Met* (1988), the last thing sixteen-year-old Drew Wingate and his fourteen-year-old sister want to do is spend two weeks on a European cruise ship with their grandmother, Connie Carlson, a jazz singer who performs on the ship. By the end of their voyage of discovery, the siblings have not only discovered many European capitals, but a lot about their family as well.

In *Unfinished Portrait of Jessica* (1991), fourteen-year-old Jessica blames her mother for her adored father's running out on them. When she is allowed to go to Mexico and spend the Christmas holidays with him, she is thrilled. Unfortunately, while Jessica travels south with dreams of being reunited with her father, her father has gone to Mexico in pursuit of a warm climate, eternal youth, and another woman. Although not what she expects, Jessica's trip allows her to discover who her father really is and what place she has in his life. She returns home to her mother sadder but wiser.

Back in the United States

After his two years in Europe, Richard Peck returned to the United States and enrolled in a masters program in English at Southern Illinois University. To pay for his education, he worked as a teaching assistant at the university. His first assignment was to teach writing to freshmen at night. Expecting a group of teens straight out of high school, he was surprised when he showed up at his first class and encountered a room full of mature adults. "I was never again to know students this vulnerable or this punctual,"[2] he later commented. Right away, Peck discovered that he enjoyed being a teacher. However, what he really longed to do was to teach young people instead of adults.

4 To Teach ... or Not to Teach

Upon receiving his master's degree in 1959, Peck continued teaching at Southern Illinois. Then, in the fall of 1961, he finally got his chance to teach kids. He was hired by a public high school in Northbrook, a wealthy suburb of Chicago. The twenty-seven-year-old teacher was shocked to discover that his students at Glenbrook North High School were nothing like the teens with whom he had grown up. Peck described his students as "armored with adolescent facades [exteriors], peer-group allegiance, hair spray, and family money . . . Every parent expected college entrance for his child. If there was an alternative, it was unthinkable."[1]

29

Peck's first impressions would remain with him long after he gave up teaching. In fact, these suburban students would serve as inspiration for the characters that would end up in many of his novels. They would also be the readers he had in mind when writing. As Peck said in *Anonymously Yours*: "Most of the letters I receive from young readers bear suburban postmarks, and most of the school-visit invitations lead me to suburbia."[2]

When Peck first began to teach, and later to write, in the United States, many families with children were moving from cities to suburbs. There was, and continues to be, a belief that life in the suburbs is problem-free, without urban concerns such as crime, poverty, racial conflict, and drugs. Yet Peck disagreed. The truth was that you can't avoid life's problems just by escaping to the suburbs. This is why his acclaimed 1976 novel, *Are You in the House Alone?*, about a high school junior who gets raped by her best friend's boyfriend, takes place in a wealthy, fictional Connecticut suburb. According to Peck it was "a setting my readers couldn't distance themselves from and deny."[3] For the same reason, *Remembering the Good Times* (1985), in which one of a trio of close friends commits suicide, is also set in a newly built suburb in which the problem of suicide is thought not to exist. And Northbrook itself would provide the setting for his tenth novel, *Close Enough to Touch* (1981), in which a teenage boy deals with the sudden death of his girlfriend.

Even in Peck's more humorous novels, the suburbs come under attack. After receiving too many letters that began "Today at the mall . . ."[4] Peck decided to go to a mall. "It was hard to grasp that home was optional, school was more optional still, but daily attendance at the mall was required,"[5] he confesses in the appropriately named autobiographical book *Love and Death at the Mall* (1994). After trailing teens around the climate-controlled halls with a notebook, amazed that they didn't pay him the slightest attention, Peck was inspired to write a satire. *Secrets of the Shopping Mall* (1979) was an ironic take on a teen fantasy in which two teens, Barnie and Teresa, run away and actually start living, full-time, in a mall.

Many readers loved this novel, and Peck hated malls so much that years later he wrote yet another mall satire, *Bel-Air Bambi and the Mall Rats* (1993). This time, however, the mall wasn't a place to escape to. A hangout for a teenage gang called the Mall Rats, it was instead a place to avoid.

In the meantime, a frustrated Peck spent two years at Glenbrook North before finally quitting to work as a textbook editor in Chicago. During his two years as an editor, he and a college friend, Norman Strasma, wrote and published a guide to Chicago nightlife. Although today Peck doesn't think much of it, *Old Town, A Complete Guide: Strolling, Shopping, Supping and Sipping* (1963), was his first published book.

Off to New York

His decision to give teaching another chance was made a lot easier by the fact that the job Peck was applying for was in the city of his dreams, New York. Hunter College High School was a cutting-edge experimental school for academically gifted girls. Part of Hunter College, it was located on Manhattan's wealthy Park Avenue. This meant that aside from being bright, Peck's English students would also be quite well-off.

In *Presenting Richard Peck* (1993), Peck recalls his first day on the job: "On the way to the first class my knees wobbled a little as they hadn't done for years. I wondered what I had to offer young geniuses flourishing in the rich cultural concrete of this world capital."[6] Unfortunately, however, teaching in the middle of Manhattan proved to be just as frustrating, if not more so, than teaching in the suburbs. According to Peck, because his students were labeled as "gifted," they felt they had nothing to learn. They weren't interested in writing. "The only writing they did with passion was on the notes they tirelessly circulated."[7]

Furthermore, they found all the books Peck assigned to be "irrelevant"[8] (useless). After much searching, Peck finally believed he had found the perfect novel to engage his students. Carson McCullers's *The Member of the Wedding* (1946) was a chronicle of the hopes and insecurities of a young teenage girl named Frankie Adams. Enthusiastically, Peck ordered a set of novels for the entire class and distributed them one Friday. The following Monday, all the books were in a pile on his desk. "We won't be reading a book about a crazy girl,"[9] announced an unofficial spokeswoman for the class.

Peck grew increasingly discouraged by unchallenging school curriculums, low academic standards, and parents who seemed absent from their children's lives. One day, in one of his classes, a girl sitting at her desk fell into the aisle, unconscious. She was taken to the hospital, where it was discovered she had overdosed on drugs. When the school called her mother, the mother thought the girl lived with her grandmother. When the school called her grandmother, the grandmother thought the girl lived with her mother.

Years later, Peck wrote a poem called "A Teacher's Prayer," which summed up many of his feelings and frustrations about teaching. The following is the poem's first stanza:

Oh God, I'm only a teacher,

And it's lonely work because I'm the only member of my species in the room.

I like kids, and I love my subject matter,

And I have higher hopes for these kids of mine than they have for themselves:

I want them to create. They want to consume.

I want them to love the world. They want the world to love them.

I want every day to be different. They want every day to be the same.

I want them to burn with zeal, about something. They want to be cool, about everything.

I want them to think. They want me to tell them.

I want the bell to ring. They want the bell to ring.[10]

Feeling frustrated by the lack of interesting and up-to-date reading material for young people, Peck decided to take matters into his own hands. With a colleague named Ned Hoopes, he compiled a book of essays by modern thinkers to be used in the classroom. The book, *Edge of Awareness: Twenty-five Contemporary Essays*, was published in 1966. It was so successful that the publisher, Dell, asked Peck to do another textbook anthology, this time a collection of contemporary poems for high school students. Published in 1970, *Sounds and Silences: Poetry for Now* was followed by another poetry collection, *Mindscapes*, which came out the following year. Both included poems written by Peck himself.

Peck continued teaching for two more years before he realized that he was burning out. At the age of thirty-seven, he quit his job and turned his back on teaching for good. His plans? To become what he had always dreamed of being—a writer.

On the evening of May 24, 1971, Richard Peck packed up his belongings and returned to his home to begin writing his first novel. At that point, home was an 1830s carriage house located in a residential alley in Brooklyn Heights, a tree-lined neighborhood of old houses that gaze across the East River toward Manhattan. He had this to say about the decision: "Though I resigned from teaching in order to write, teaching is a job you never really quit. You just go on and on, trying to turn life into lesson plans."[11]

5 A Big Gamble

Oddly, if he hadn't first been a teacher, Richard Peck probably never would have become a successful young adult novelist. His teaching experiences provided him with two crucial things: subject matter to write about and an audience to write for—high school and junior high students.

He also learned that although puberty was the age at which most kids turn their backs on reading, this is when they most need novels. He had learned firsthand how teens dressed, talked, and acted among themselves. He had also learned (though often the hard way) what they look for in a book: to be entertained and reassured. And even then, he knew that only a certain kind of teen would ever be likely to pick up a book he wrote. According to Peck, these were "the thoughtful, quiet ones—students who will reach for a book in search of themselves—who often get overlooked in our crisis-oriented society and the schools that mirror it."[1] With all these "lessons" in mind, Peck carried his manual typewriter out into his backyard and began writing his first novel, *Don't Look and It Won't Hurt.*

While fishing around for an interesting subject, Peck remembered the young pregnant girls he had met at the house of his friends, the Hugheses. Richard Hughes was a doctor who lived in Evanston, Illinois. He and his wife, Jean, took in unmarried pregnant girls, providing them with a home until they gave birth. Peck had met some of these girls and was curious about their stories. The Hugheses said that all the girls who stayed with them vowed never to return home. Instead, they hoped to keep their babies and marry the fathers. However, once they had actually given birth, all of the girls did give up their babies and return home to their families. The fathers rarely entered the picture.

With this information, Peck was ready to start his novel. Yet immediately, a big problem

arose. When he began to write from the point
of view of the pregnant teen, he got stuck.
Somehow Ellen, the unwed mother, could not or
would not tell her own story. Starting over, Peck
decided to tell seventeen-year-old Ellen's story
from the viewpoint of her younger sister, Carol.

Fifteen-year-old Carol is the middle sister
in a poor family of three girls whose father
lives across town. While her mother works all
the time, Carol takes care of her little sister,
Liz. She also becomes the confidante of Ellen,
who falls for a twenty-year-old drug dealer.
When her boyfriend is arrested and sent to jail,
Ellen confesses to Carol that she is pregnant.
Having fought with her mother, Ellen leaves
the small town of Claypitts for Chicago.
Waiting to have her baby, she is taken in by a
kind family to whom she becomes attached.
Meanwhile, Carol is the only one with whom
Ellen stays in touch.

Carol spends most of the novel trying to keep
her fragmented family together. Fearing Ellen
will never come back home, she bravely sneaks
away to Chicago, hoping to convince her sister
to return once she has given up her baby. Typical
of a Richard Peck novel—and of life itself,
according to Peck—the ending is not happy and

many loose ends are left unresolved. For instance, we don't see Ellen have her baby. Neither do we know if she really will return home. The one thing that has changed, however, is Carol. The problems she has had to deal with, the responsibilities she was forced to take on, and the journey she was brave enough to make have all made her grow up.

The novel's last chapter begins with the end of her journey:

> "Well Mom, I'm back." Nervous as I was, I was still proud I'd done it . . .
> "Well, how were things up there?"
> "You mean Ellen, Mom?"
> "Yes, Ellen."
> "She's a little confused now, but I think she'll be all right. I think we'll get her back."
> "Well, if we do, it's you that saw to it. I couldn't have managed it. I wanted to do something myself, but I didn't know how . . ."
> I headed off toward town then, feeling like I was just back from a trip around the world.[2]

The four months it took to write *Don't Look and It Won't Hurt* were difficult ones. Peck was unemployed and single, with no one to support him. While he wrote his novel, he was so afraid of spending the little money he had that he rarely left the house. In truth, Peck was taking a big gamble.

Fortunately, it was a gamble that paid off. Although Peck had never written fiction, the books of collected essays and poems he had put together while he was still teaching at Hunter had given him important contacts in New York's publishing world. One such contact was George Nicholson, then editor-in-chief of juvenile books at the publisher Holt, Rinehart & Winston. Upon finishing the sixth draft of *Don't Look and It Won't Hurt*, Peck placed his manuscript in a shoe box and took it to George Nicholson's office. The next day, Peck's phone rang. It was George Nicholson telling Peck that he could begin his second novel.

Don't Look and It Won't Hurt would go on to sell more than half a million copies, and in 1992 it would inspire the independent film *Gas Food Lodging*. Meanwhile, critical reaction to the novel was largely positive. A review in *Publishers Weekly* described it as "an extraordinarily good"[3] first novel, while a reviewer in *Booklist* stated that it was "real and affecting."[4]

Other People's Lives

Many authors of fiction for both young adults and adults draw on their own lives for inspiration in their writing. This is often especially true for their first books. Richard Peck, however, has always been dead set against the autobiographical novel, in which the main character is the writer himself, thinly disguised. As such, none of the characters in a Richard Peck book are anything like Peck. Similarly, none of his characters' problems or situations are ones he has experienced himself.

Instead, Peck's novels are the result of a great deal of observation and research. In fact, Peck compares writing a novel to making a patchwork quilt: "You gather bright scraps from other people's lives, and then you stitch them together in a pattern of your own."[5] Peck has always been more interested in other people's lives than in his own. He gets many ideas from "memories, usually of other people, even other people's memories."[6] He also gets ideas from other people's books. As he says, "We're always looking to other people for our stories, then creating other people to tell them."[7] Peck also loves reading his colleagues' young adult novels to keep up with what's going on in what he considers to be the most exciting field in publishing.

6 Problem Solving

As he started work on his second novel, *Dreamland Lake* (1973), Peck supported himself by taking on other writing assignments. He wrote articles on travel, local history, and architecture for the *New York Times*, and he published articles in magazines. However, financial security was less of a concern for Peck than the sudden loneliness of being a writer. As he put it, "Teaching . . . hadn't taught me how to sit alone in an empty room without bells. I missed the shape of the school day. I missed colleagues and young voices."[1]

During the writing of *Don't Look and It Won't Hurt* and Peck's next two novels, *Dreamland Lake* and *Through a Brief Darkness* (1973), Peck could still clearly recall the faces of the students he used to teach. He could easily remember their chatter, and what they had and had not responded to in the books he'd assigned for them to read. But as time passed, the students' "faces began to fade, and their voices echoed away into silence."[2] Moreover, Peck observed that while he "was growing older every minute at the typewriter, [his] readers remained mysteriously the same age."[3]

Following the publication of his first novel, Peck was requested to speak to groups of librarians and teachers, and he was also invited by schools all over the United States to read from his books and discuss them with students. Peck loved the experience of being out among his readers, interacting with them and seeing what made them tick. As he said, "I fell for public speaking just as I'd fallen for teaching . . . Being a writer was to take me far from the house in the alley, and to fulfill that other early dream of going everywhere. I was going to see classrooms and school libraries in places I'd never heard of, and find ideas that I could never have thought of. It would be teaching without tears. I [didn't] have to grade anybody."[4]

Rise of the YA Novel

Interestingly, the time at which Peck began his writing career coincided with the rise of a specific youth culture in North America. Up until the social and cultural revolutions of the 1960s, society had largely viewed adolescence as a temporary transitional phase between childhood and adulthood. However, in the late 1960s, teens as a group began to develop a voice and identity of their own. It was suddenly discovered that teens had habits that differed from those of children and adults, as well as their own specific likes and dislikes, behavior and fashions, and their own specific problems. Novels began to appear that were written especially for them. This new literary category—young adult (YA) fiction—focused on adolescent problems and characters, and these books were written in a style and language used by contemporary young people themselves.

One of the first and most important examples of a YA novel was written by a teenage girl from Tulsa, Oklahoma, named S. E. Hinton. Hinton wrote *The Outsiders* in 1967, while she herself was still in high school. Her book captured a real teen's parentless world of peer pressure, gangs, and violence. A great success, *The Outsiders* shone a light on teen issues and helped open the door to a whole new field of publishing.

Along with writers such as Robert Lipsyte (*The Contender*, 1967), Paul Zindel (*The Pigman*, 1968),

John Donovan (*I'll Get There. It Better Be Worth the Trip*, 1969), M. E. Kerr (*Dinky Hocker Shoots Smack*, 1972), Norma Klein (*Mom, the Wolfman and Me*, 1972), and Robert Cormier (*The Chocolate War*, 1974), Richard Peck was one of the pioneers of YA fiction. In their attempts to write relevant books that young people could identify with and learn from, many YA authors wrote what later became classified as teen "problem novels."

Problem novels boldly tackled tough issues such as drugs and divorce, rape and racism, often for the first time. During the 1970s and 1980s this genre, or category, of novel became very popular. Unfortunately, some books made the mistake of dealing with a single issue in a simplistic, preachy manner. They featured unbelievable characters and unbelievable endings that were difficult for young readers to identify with. A few, however, such as those written by the authors mentioned above, were realistic, multidimensional stories. They boasted complex characters whose problems were not always completely solved by the novels' ends. Peck's novels were considered among the best of these "because they deal with multiple problems and they are so artfully written."[5]

Are You in the House Alone?

One of Peck's first, most influential, and best-selling problem novels was *Are You in the House Alone?* Published in 1976, it is still considered one of the best and most sensitive YA novels to deal with rape. In tackling such a serious issue, Peck conducted a lot of research. At a rape crisis center, he interviewed doctors, lawyers, police officers, and rape victims. As he said in an interview, "I wanted my readers to know some things about this crime, that our laws are stacked against the victim and in favor of the criminal. I wanted them to know some of the medical aspects of this problem, and I also wanted them to know what it's like to be a victim."[6]

The victim and main protagonist of *Are You in the House Alone?* is Gail, a seemingly happy sixteen-year-old girl. Gail and her family feel safe and sound in their wealthy suburban home. When she begins receiving menacing notes and phone calls, she follows the advice of her best friend, Alison, and tries to pretend that none of this increasingly scary stuff is happening. Unfortunately, it is, and Gail is so naive and unsuspecting that she opens the door and lets her rapist—a boy from a good family who goes to her school—into the house.

That the actual rape scene is not depicted in the novel (Gail is knocked unconscious) is significant. As Peck himself stated, the novel isn't about rape. "Young readers already know what that is. Instead it points out that life is not a television show with justice neatly delivered just before the final commercial."[7] After Gail is raped, her ordeal, like the novel, isn't over; it's only just beginning. The novel deals realistically with how a rape victim is treated, not only by the medical and legal professions, but also by her friends and family. Most of these, like Alison, either blame Gail or, like her mother, try to pretend this horrible event never happened. True to life, the ending is bittersweet. On one hand, Gail emerges as a strong survivor and her maturity has brought her closer to her family. However, every day at school she risks running into the boy that raped her, who goes unpunished.

Peck worried that the touchy subject matter might harm his career. But critics praised the novel calling it "honest and perceptive,"[8] "sensitive and tasteful,"[9] and "neither sensational nor pornographic."[10]

Young readers liked the novel, too. But while it is one of Peck's most widely read books, the author has received many letters from readers claiming that he got the ending wrong. Apparently, Hollywood thought so, too. When it was made into a television movie in 1978, the script had Gail luring her rapist to the high school darkroom, where she was able to photograph him as he was about to attack her again. Peck, who had not been consulted about the film, was horrified by the tacked-on happy ending, whose moral seemed to be "keep your camera ready and hope your attacker doesn't mind providing evidence at his own trial."[11]

Fathers and Sons

Reading the adult novel *Ordinary People* (1976), by Judith Guest gave Peck the idea for his next problem novel, *Father Figure* (1978). *Ordinary People* is about a well-off suburban family that is torn apart by guilt and grief when the oldest son dies in a boating accident. While the mother retreats into herself, the father and surviving son awkwardly try to forge an emotional bond.

Father Figure features Jim, the novel's seventeen-year-old protagonist, and his younger brother. When their mother grows sick, Jim becomes a father figure to eight-year-old Byron. Following her death, the two brothers travel to Florida and struggle to build a relationship with their father, who had abandoned the family eight years earlier. Resentful of his father and protective of his brother, Jim must make a tough adult decision: He must leave Byron in his father's care while he goes back to finish high school in New York. At the novel's end, before he leaves for New York, father and son try cautiously to lay the beginnings of a future relationship.

A review in *Publishers Weekly* said the novel was "assuredly one of the best [novels] for all ages in many a moon."[12] *Father Figure* was also made into a television movie. Peck was pleased with the film, not only because his ending was left unchanged, but because of the strong performance given by the twenty-year-old actor Timothy Hutton, who played Jim. Coincidentally, the following year, Hutton would win an Academy Award for his role as the surviving son in the film version of *Ordinary People*.

A Rare Kind of Romance

In talking with teens and publishers, Peck learned that young people liked love stories. After a seventh grader at a Toronto school asked if he had written anything on dating, Peck decided to try his hand at romance. The novel he would end up writing, *Close Enough to Touch*, is not the fluffy soap opera-style romance his readers were probably expecting. Instead, it is a teen romance told from a boy's point of view—which is extremely rare. Peck admits that he wrote the book "to give boys an emotional voice." As he says, "Now I get letters from girls who want to meet the boy."[13] In fact, Peck wanted to deal with male perspectives, feelings, and relationships, particularly the often hard-to-express bonds between fathers and sons. Concerned that many boys don't know how to express their emotions, Peck has created narrator-protagonists such as Jim, Matt (the hero of *Close Enough to Touch*), and *Remembering the Good Times'* Buck who, according to one critic, are "some of the most sensitive male characters in all of young adult literature."[14]

Close Enough to Touch is also unusual in that it begins with the sudden death of Dory, Matt's girlfriend. Instead of depicting a passionate romance, most of the novel focuses on how Matt deals with grief and loss as well as with the reactions of his classmates in junior high. In the novel, conflicts stem from the fact that Matt is poor while his schoolmates are from wealthy families. Moreover, most of his friends were actually Dory's cliquey friends, who snub him after she is dead. Fortunately, on hand to help Matt deal with his emotions are his father, stepmother, grandmother, and an outspoken, nonconformist senior, Margaret, whom he begins to romance at the end of the novel.

The *Bulletin of the Center for Children's Books* called *Close Enough To Touch* "compelling and bittersweet."[16] A review in the *ALAN Review* (published by the Assembly on Literature for Adolescents of the National Council of Teachers of English) admitted that the novel "could have leaned towards the maudlin [overly sentimental] except for Peck's superb infusion of humor and his emphatic, yet unsentimental, tone."[17]

A Life and Death Issue

A more upsetting response to the novel came when Peck went traveling to schools to talk about it. When discussing how a boy in Matt's situation could deal with the death of his girlfriend, Peck was shocked by what he heard. In almost every classroom, a boy suggested that Matt could solve his problems by killing himself. After he visited one seventh-grade classroom where three boys had committed suicide in one year, Peck was stunned. Immediately, he began what he called "painful"[18] research into the causes and warning signs of teenage suicide, which was, at the time— 1985—responsible for the death of one young American every ninety minutes. He discovered that suicide victims were often boys, most often high achievers from comfortable backgrounds. Under immense pressure from parents, teachers, and society as a whole to succeed, they also felt they lacked the necessary skills to do so.

The knowledge Peck gained from his research led to the novel *Remembering the Good Times,* in which Trav Kirby, a brilliant but uptight and overly serious boy who constantly drives himself, ends up committing suicide. However, instead of focusing on Trav's suicide and its effects on those left behind, Peck chose to tell it as the story of a friendship.

The friendship between Trav, beautiful and strong-minded Kate, and narrator Buck, the most observant, if sometimes most uncomprehending of the three, is a particularly close one. It begins when the characters are twelve years old and continues until they are sixteen. This four-year time span allows readers to become involved with the characters. It also gives them enough time to observe the subtle clues that Trav leaves behind, clues that those around him overlook until it is too late. In the end, Trav's suicide comes as a shock to both characters and readers alike.

The novel doesn't end with Trav's death, but with Kate and Buck learning to move on without him. Peck points out:

A suicide victim can't be a protagonist for young readers, because the book must be the biography of a survivor . . . This becomes the heart of the matter, because Kate's a girl who's always believed that every problem has a solution, and Buck is a boy who hasn't given himself permission to cry . . . even a novel about a boy who kills himself has to be, somehow, better, more hopeful, than real life.[19]

Author and critic Michael Cart noted that *Remembering the Good Times* is not only "a fine and important book . . . [that] successfully dramatizes a vital issue,"[20] but also one that "is beautifully written, full of memorable lines and moments."[21] As an example, he points to Peck's description of the bully who beats up Buck, wearing "year-long overalls and a sweat shirt. It looked like the sleeves of it had been bitten off by wild beasts."[22]

Other critics praised the novel for its "quiet intensity,"[23] "finely honed style,"[24] and the fact that "all the characters shimmer."[25] *Publishers Weekly* called it Peck's "best book so far."[26] Peck himself is of the same opinion. At various moments, including during the interview featured in the back of this book, Peck has declared *Remembering the Good Times* to be the best novel he has written to date.

7 Remembering the Good Times

Just as important to Peck as his school and library visits are the letters he receives from young readers. As he puts it, "The mail delivery looms large when it brings the only human voice all day."[1] Peck divides his reader mail into two types. There are the letters assigned by teachers, some of which begin: "Our teacher told us to write to our favorite author, and I'm the only one in the room writing to you," or even "Our teacher told us to write to our favorite author. Could you please get me the address of Danielle Steel?"[2] However, there are also the letters from kids who wanted to write them. According to Peck, these letters often come in the summertime, "from people thoughtful enough, and lonely enough"[3] to write to him. They write because one of Peck's novels moved them or because they identify strongly with a character, or recognize a place. They write to complain that he got the ending wrong or to demand a sequel. Directly or indirectly, they often steer the author in new directions and provide him with ideas for future novels.

In 1974, Peck had just completed his fourth novel, *Representing Super Doll*, and he wanted a change from writing about contemporary teen issues in contemporary teen settings. He had recently received a letter from a boy asking him to write a ghost story. He agreed to do so, but with a slight twist. Instead of being spooky or scary, Peck's ghost story would be funny. "I'd rather write comedy than not,"[4] Peck has confessed, and even the most serious of his novels include some moments of humor. This new novel would also focus on one of Peck's favorite themes: the relationship between an inexperienced young person and an older, wiser one.

The Birth of Blossom Culp

Set in the early 1900s, *The Ghost Belonged to Me* is set in a small Midwest town called Bluff City that was based on Peck's hometown of Decatur. Peck drew on many of his relatives' stories to conjure up Bluff City and its eccentric residents. Their voices and speech patterns found their way into the book as did Peck's much-loved great uncle Miles. However, it is neither the eccentric Miles, nor his ghost-seeing nephew, Alexander (who is the book's hero) that made *The Ghost Belonged to Me* so popular with readers and critics alike. As Peck recalls, "As I wrote, I saw I'd created a young boy, an old man, and a dead girl. I liked them, but they were all too apart from one another . . . Worried now, I took the character of Huckleberry Finn and gave him a sex change. Then I looked up from my typewriter and saw a girl standing in the door of my New York study. Her name was Blossom Culp, and she's never left it."[5]

Blossom is the poorest, ugliest, clumsiest, loneliest, biggest mess of a girl in Bluff City. Abandoned by her drunken father, she lives on the wrong side of the tracks with her toothless witch of a mother who spends most of her time reading tea leaves. In spite of the fact that so much is against her, Blossom is full of humor, courage, and determination—like most of Peck's female protagonists. It's been said that she "ranks among the spunkiest characters in contemporary literature for children and young adults."[6] Aside from "the talent for involving [her]self in other people's business,"[7] which frequently gets her into trouble, Blossom is also able to see into the future. And, she is quite adept at time travel.

Blossom Culp was such a popular character that following the novel's publication, Peck was flooded by readers' letters addressed to her. About her popularity, a surprised but pleased Peck commented that "Her clothes are wrong; her speech is wrong; she takes no orders from the peer group; and [she's] become by far my most loved character."[8] From the reaction to Blossom, Peck learned that his young readers were willing to identify in a book "with the very people they snub and punish in real life."[9]

Since she was so well received, Blossom became the main protagonist and narrator of the next three novels Peck wrote featuring the supernatural adventures of Alexander and Blossom Culp—*Ghosts I Have Been* (1977), *The Dreadful Future of Blossom Culp* (1983), and *Blossom Culp and the Sleep of Death* (1986). These time-traveling escapades were considerable successes and critics overwhelmingly agreed with *School Library Journal*'s view of Blossom as "a thoroughly engaging heroine."[10]

Modern Times

After *Blossom Culp and the Sleep of Death*—the last Blossom Culp book—Peck's writing increasingly dealt with time travel and the past, often mixing fantasy and humor with a hint of nostalgia for the kind of "good old days" he grew up listening to stories about. *Voices After Midnight* (1989), is a comedy about a California family that moves to an old house in New York City. Depending on their moods and the doors they open, the family members find themselves in the year 1888. *Lost in Cyberspace* (1995) and its sequel, *The Great Interactive Dream Machine* (1996), are a mixture of time travel and computer technology that feature sixth-grader Josh Lewis and his best friend, Aaron, who travel through cyberspace into the past. Both books are a testament to Peck's research capacity and ability to keep up-to-date with his readers.

In truth, the author is so stubbornly opposed to computer technology that he insists on typing his novels on an electric typewriter. This detail sums up much about Richard Peck. While he has a sincere passion for young people and has built a very successful career out of capturing the many elements of their world, he is, at the same time, very critical of much about contemporary society, particularly about contemporary youth behavior and culture.

Teens who spend all day in front of a TV or computer or shopping in a suburban mall, who blame their parents for their problems, or who walk around blindly in cliques are treated roughly in a Richard Peck novel. Then again, so are the many other factors in today's society that Peck holds responsible for the state of today's teens: unchallenging academic programs, teachers who are babysitters, parents who are absent from their children's lives, and a materialistic culture obsessed with what people buy and wear.

Fittingly, when Blossom is flash-forwarded in time to the present in *The Dreadful Future of Blossom Culp*, she is confused by a suburban world where computer games, Doritos, and Adidas reign. Ultimately, she finds contemporary America an interesting place to visit, but is almost immediately homesick for 1914.

Looking Back

As he grows older, Peck, like his father before him, increasingly seems to be looking back fondly at a golden past that he can share with his readers. In his novels, the past is usually played out in a small rural town somewhere in the Midwest. And the time described is around the turn of the century—back in the days of his parents' and grandparents' youth.

Aside from the Blossom Culp books, the turn of the century is also the setting for *Fair Weather*

(2001). This, Peck's most recent novel to date, takes place in 1893. Amid much historical detail, it narrates the adventures of an Illinois farm family that is invited by a lonely, widowed aunt to visit the many marvels of Chicago's World Fair.

Two more of Peck's recent novels are also set in this golden past. Despite it being the Depression, life is much more entertaining than bleak when Joey and his sister Mary Alice leave Chicago to spend part of the summer with their Grandma Dowdel. Although at first they think they are being dumped by their parents, over a period spanning various summers the siblings come to look forward to their annual trips. Not only do they have some comic adventures, but they also discover a lot about their gruff, no-nonsense, catfish-poaching, rifle-toting grandmother, who stands as Peck's reply "to all those cloying little old ladies nodding by the fire in traditional children's picture books."[11] Grandma Dowdel's fiercely independent nature is revealed in the following exchange with her grandson Joey, in *A Long Way from Chicago*:

> "Grandma," I said, "is trapping fish legal in this state?"
>
> "If it was," she said, "we wouldn't have to be so quiet."

"What's the fine?"
"Nothin' if you don't get caught."[12]

Indeed, Peck claims that Grandma Dowdel was such a strong character that it took "two books to contain [her]."[13] *A Long Way from Chicago* (1998) was followed by *A Year Down Yonder* (2000), in which a fifteen-year-old Mary Alice returns on her own to spend a year with Grandma Dowdel. Critics loved both books' "true storyteller's wit, humor, and rhythm,"[14] and they singled out the character of Grandma Dowdel—"a formidable woman whose ungrandmotherly ways are a constant source of surprise (and often shock) to her Chicago-bred grandchildren."[15]

Peck himself liked Grandma Dowdel so much that he wished she had been his grandmother. He had this to say about her: "Once or twice, perhaps, in a long writing career, a character lifts off the page and takes on extraordinary life. It happened to me many years and books ago in a character named Blossom Culp. Now it's happened again . . . And by the way . . . Grandma Dowdel's first name is Blossom."[16]

And Grandma Dowdel is only one of the latest of many elderly characters who, from the beginning of Peck's career, have played an important role in his fiction. Beginning with Uncle Miles in *The Ghost Belonged to Me,* all his novels have featured an elderly character, most often a grandmother. Not only do they offer young characters and readers a link to the past, they also function as anchors to the constantly shifting world that teens are faced with. Says Peck:

> I need them. Young readers need them more. The old folks . . . provide wisdom and seasoning won only through long lifetimes, and compassion unavailable from the peer group. They offer alternatives in the accelerating battle between parents and children, and glimpses of the problems and sorrows of old age for a young generation fixated on their own.[17]

One of his most memorable elderly characters and one whom Peck himself likes enormously is Polly Prior, Kate's grandmother in *Remembering the Good Times*. Peck himself has described her as "Blossom Culp grown old."[18] Unsurprisingly, it is in her old farmhouse, in the midst of a pear orchard, that Polly, Kate, Trav, and Buck share the book's most frequent, and best, "good times," far from the chaos of school and the rapidly developing suburbs. As author and critic Michael Cart points out, "Peck's vision of paradise" is a world where "elderly people are valued . . . and where teenagers and octogenarians can be friends and companions who care about each other."[19]

8 Writing and Reading

Sitting down to begin a new novel is always a bit tricky for Richard Peck. He is not a morning person. Instead, he says he does his best work between 4:30 PM and 6:30 PM, when everyone else is stuck in traffic between work and home.

The Writing Process

Beginning a novel is often slow work for Peck. Yet as he gets further into the story, his enthusiasm picks up, as does the pace of his writing. While he is immersed in writing, his life revolves around the fictional world he is creating. He usually begins with an idea or theme and then starts constructing the characters. Interestingly, at least half of his novels' main protagonists, in whose voices the stories are told, are girls. Moreover, his heroines are often much more independent, outspoken, and fearless than the boys with whom they share page space.

Peck is very careful about how he describes his characters. He works in references to everything from the junk food they eat and the clothes they wear to the videos they rent and the music they listen to so that readers will recognize the people in his books as "one of them." However, what really brings these characters to life is their realistic dialogue, which, for Peck, is the most fun part of writing a book. He says, "When I'm coming to a scene of conversation, then I feel as if I'm going to a party."[1] Peck claims that this enjoyment probably comes from memories of eavesdropping on adult conversations as a child. It's a habit he's continued. Whether riding around on buses or walking through a mall, he is always jotting down the conversations he overhears.

Before he has written and rewritten a novel to his satisfaction, nobody gets an advanced viewing of a Richard Peck manuscript. However, if he has doubts about a certain scene, he might read a passage aloud to a group of students at a school or library in order to get their feedback.

When a novel is finally published, there is also the issue of critics to deal with. Throughout his career, most reviewers have heaped praise and compliments upon Peck's work. Yet, on occasion, he has been accused of being too didactic (teacher-like) or of letting his own critical adult voice seep into that of his characters. Nonetheless, Peck doesn't let reviewers affect him too much. He argues that they are the wrong age for his books and he isn't writing for them, anyway. Ultimately, the reaction he cares about most is that of his young readers.

Aside from critics, Peck has had to deal with the adults, usually parents, who have tried to censor his books. In 1985, Peck was shocked when a well-to-do doctor's wife in a "picture perfect"[2] American town not only prohibited her thirteen-year-old daughter from reading *Father Figure*, but had it removed from the school library. She disapproved of the divorce of Jim's parents and she felt that Jim's disrespect for his father and his father's failure to be a good parent to him set a bad example for young readers.

However, the novels that have come under censors' most frequent fire have been the Blossom Culp books. Peck has stated that Blossom's comic adventures "have placed her and me on the forbidden book list of a powerful wave of censors splendidly organized nationwide."[3] According to Peck, a newspaper critic named Phyllis Schlafly was responsible for putting his Blossom Culp novels on this list of censored books. Schlafly warned that reading both *Ghosts I Have Been* and *The Ghost Belonged to Me* encouraged children to communicate with the dead in order to become interesting people.

Although he feels he is in good company—in recent years other banned books have ranged from *The Diary of Anne Frank* and Robert Cormier's *The Chocolate War* (1974) to Aldous Huxley's *Brave New World* (1932) and Shakespeare's *The Merchant of Venice* (c. 1600)—Peck has fought back against book censors and is a fierce supporter of young people's right to read. Unsurprisingly, his outrage against censorship and the fundamentalist beliefs that fuel some of it made their way into a recent novel, *The Last Safe Place on Earth* (1995).

In the novel, fifteen-year-old Todd Tobin and his family live on Tranquility Lane, in the well-off suburb of Walden Woods. When Laurel, a good-looking girl from school whom Todd has a crush on, is hired to baby-sit his little sister Marnie, Todd is pretty excited. The last thing he and his tight-knit family expect is that Laurel will turn out to be a Christian fundamentalist who scares Marnie to death with some extreme ideas. Not only does she equate Halloween trick-or-treating with devil worship, but her mother is a book banner who calls "that Anne Frank book [*The Diary of Anne Frank*] . . . unchristian."[4]

Peck wrote *The Last Safe Place on Earth* because he feels that so many of his readers don't know that "they have freedom of speech." As Peck says, "I'm not sure their peer group leaders give them freedom of speech . . . I wanted to ask young people, young readers, where they stood in the censorship wars."[5] This direct approach is typical of Peck, whose goal as an author is to challenge his readers by writing "novels that ask honest questions about serious issues; a novel is never an answer, it's always a question."[6] Because in the last ten years public libraries and, to a greater extent, school libraries have come under increasingly heavy attack from organized book banners, Peck feels that censorship, reading, and kids' right to read is something they themselves should be thinking and talking about.

If Peck defends both writing and reading so passionately, it is because he sees both as important ways of discovering one's self, of finding one's own voice, and of creating one's own independent identity. Books allow young people to both create and discover new worlds. This is a lesson Peck himself learned and one he is determined to pass on to future generations. He is clearly depressed by the fact that fewer young people seem to be reading than ever before, but if he can reach just one young person through his writing, he will feel as if he has accomplished something. Says Peck: "I caught my first glimpses of the world and the future in books. Here in some other century I hope young readers still do."[7]

Interview with Richard Peck

ANNIE SOMMERS: Many of your novels are set in the past or involve some form of time travel. If you yourself could travel in time, where would you go and why?

RICHARD PECK: I always said that spiritually, I wish I had died in the First World War. That would have been my period. I love that turning of the last century, that wonderful sense of innovation and progress of that time. We have more innovations now but less drama.

ANNIE SOMMERS: What would you like to have done during that time period?

RICHARD PECK: Oh, nothing at all, of course. Just do what I do now. Just go around asking people questions. What would I like to do? Oh, be king of England, how's that?

ANNIE SOMMERS: That's good. Which, if any of your young adult novels have meant the most to you, and for what reason?

RICHARD PECK: That's a good question. Of course, the novel that means the most to me is always the next one, isn't it? But the one of the past that means the most is *Remembering the Good Times*. It's the best book I can do, and it was the hardest to write, and it has elicited the most meaningful letters from young readers. And that's the important thing.

ANNIE SOMMERS: Meaningful in what way?

RICHARD PECK: Making contact with them, hearing them say, "You're writing about what happened here."

ANNIE SOMMERS: Usually, many of your protagonists are girls. Why is this, and do you think it's more difficult for a male author to get inside a female's head, or are there any secrets?

RICHARD PECK: I go back and forth between male and female characters . . . protagonists, because of course I want readers of both genders . . . girls and women are easier to research than men because girls and women are more open in their discussions of emotions and relationships. And novels are about emotions and relationships. With boys and men you have to interpret, often through the metaphor of sports or warfare or something else, whereas girls are much more open on this subject. I also notice they are much more open in their writing on this subject. I look at a lot of student writing. It's one of my sources.

ANNIE SOMMERS: How has your writing changed over the years?

RICHARD PECK: I often think I haven't learned a thing about writing after thirty novels. When I'm working on the next one I say, "I don't know how to do this one." But I think probably having written those novels does help. I guess I'm aware now that I'm going to have to write it six times. I'm sure any writer will tell you that it doesn't get easier, in fact.

ANNIE SOMMERS: It probably gets harder.

RICHARD PECK: Yeah, I have to keep stopping to say, "Have I written this before? Am I repeating myself? That line sounded too good. I must have said it before." Things like that. On the other hand, I think you do learn more about the shaping of a novel by having done it. It just doesn't feel as if it's getting any easier.

ANNIE SOMMERS: Which of your characters would you most like to have lunch with in real life?

RICHARD PECK: Well, I'm not sure . . . Blossom Culp has been very good to me over the years. I'm not sure I want to take her to lunch. And

Grandma Dowdel has changed my life. I'm not sure I want to take her to lunch.

ANNIE SOMMERS: What if they took you to lunch? Or what if you could watch them have lunch? Be in the next room and watch through invisible glass?

RICHARD PECK: (laughs) Yeah, that's what writing is. Always being at the next table.

ANNIE SOMMERS: So you wouldn't want to have lunch with them?

RICHARD PECK: Writers are people who don't have lunch with people. They sit next to those people . . .

ANNIE SOMMERS: You receive a lot of mail from readers. What do you do with it all and can you remember one of the most memorable or treasured letters that you've received?

RICHARD PECK: Well, I do have a letter that still haunts me, and it's about *Remembering the Good Times*; *Remembering the Good Times* being a novel that dramatizes the classic warning signs of teenage suicide, in the hope that young readers will see things that parents don't and go for help for a friend perhaps. And I got a letter about that book that said, "The only trouble with your book is I didn't find it in time." I think that's a letter that still . . . is still with me.

ANNIE SOMMERS: What do you think is the biggest problem facing today's young people that you would like to tackle in an upcoming novel?

RICHARD PECK: I probably wouldn't. I have turned away from contemporary issues but I guess there is an answer to that one, and that is I think this last year has indicated that we have been crippled as a society because we know no history. So we have to keep repeating it. And so I am committed now to the historical novel. Though in the past I started out writing con-temporary novels on immediate issues, as so many of us in the YA field did in the 1970s. All these issues were suddenly surfacing. Now the issues seem to me that the young have no sense of the past. They don't know when the Civil War was. They don't know who we fought in World War II.

ANNIE SOMMERS: Although your novels include many romances between young people, you almost never deal with sexual relations.

RICHARD PECK: No, I don't. And also, I don't deal much with romance, unless I can turn it into a comedy. I don't believe much in romance under thirty. I think it's confusion, not romance. But I have very little sexual content in my books, probably because I was a teacher. And partly because I know now that I will be censored somewhere for anything I write. But they're not going to get me on that. They're going to have to dig more deeply to ban me. Also, I don't write about sexual situations because I get very little information about that from young readers, young people. I have had many, many thousands of letters over thirty years and not one of them has mentioned the subject of sex or the subject of conformity, the two issues that perhaps are the most important in their lives.

ANNIE SOMMERS: You just feel that it's not something you want to write about . . .

RICHARD PECK: Yeah, although my best-selling novel for many years was *Are You in the House Alone?*, which is about a rape victim, but it wasn't about the rape, it was about what we do to victims. And now we have another book, by Laurie Halse Anderson, called *Speak*, on the same issue. And it's very interesting to me to see how she handles the same issue these twenty-five years later.

ANNIE SOMMERS: You've said that you never begin to grow up until you declare your independence from your peers. Does this mean that you can envision, for example, a grade nine where there aren't any cliques or where everybody's an individual? Do you think that that could actually be possible?

RICHARD PECK: No, it isn't possible. You have to take independent action. In my teaching, I noticed nobody ever grew up in a group. You can hide in a group. You can be organized in a group. But the group impedes change. Whereas, if you're going to change and move forward, you're going to have to do it on your own.

ANNIE SOMMERS: Do you still have a cat?

RICHARD PECK: I used to. Cats stalk through a lot of my stories. Dogs, too. But I don't now because I travel so much I can't manage it. But I miss a cat.

ANNIE SOMMERS: Did the cat influence your writing in any way?

RICHARD PECK: Oh yeah. Cats are writers' best friends. They are another presence in the room who do not have to go for walks.

ANNIE SOMMERS: You really listen to young readers and students and that seems unique.

RICHARD PECK: It just flowed so directly from teaching for me. And nobody can teach you how to be a writer, but you can take the courses to become a teacher. Actually, you can't be taught to be a teacher, either. You learn both these trades when you're already on the job and the door is closed between you and all help . . . When I was teaching, I was always looking at material, saying "How do I present this to my students? What are they going to think about this? How can I break down their resistance to this? How can I light a fire here?" And the idea that you wouldn't keep going back to them just seems impossible to me because then I wouldn't know how to write. Also, writing's lonely, and I miss the companionship of teaching. And not everybody has taught, although a lot of us have . . . Teaching for me was a vastly uncentering experience. I didn't have time for my problems, and nobody was interested in them.

ANNIE SOMMERS: It must have been kind of liberating, in a way.

RICHARD PECK: It was. It liberated me to write, in fact. I don't think I would have been a writer . . .

ANNIE SOMMERS: If you hadn't taught?

RICHARD PECK: No, I don't think so. I wanted to be a writer long before I was grown, but I don't think I would have made it without teaching. I credit teaching with that.

ANNIE SOMMERS: And why did you want to be a writer?

RICHARD PECK: My mother read to me before I could read. That was it. Those were more interesting worlds than mine. I still think it. We still think all the things we thought at five. I can remember saying, "Oh, when I go to school next year I'll be able to read these books for myself." If I could give kids any gift it would be that.

ANNIE SOMMERS: I know that Robert Cormier was a great influence on you?

RICHARD PECK: Oh, I think he was. I looked up to him a great deal. I think we need our idols. And now I am of the age in which I am looking at younger writers, you see. And I love the work of Will Hobbs. I just don't think anybody does it the way he does it. He can use the Western American settings without ever dwarfing the characters. And that's a piece of brilliance. It's hard to do. I write about the indoors. He writes about the outdoors. And so I'll go anywhere his novels say. I think he's one of our best. Also in that vein, Graham Salisbury is somebody whose work I look forward to. His short story collection, *Island Boyz,* is just a treasure, and how he deals with all of the different languages of Hawaii and how he uses a setting in his own distinct way, takes you to a place you haven't been. His first book, *Blue Skin of the Sea*, I love, and his book that just won the *Boston Globe/Horn Book* Award this year, *Lord of the Deep* . . . These are two writers who are just such clear indication that this field just keeps getting better.

ANNIE SOMMERS: Is there an award that has meant the most to you in a particular way?

RICHARD PECK: Well, first of all, we don't write for awards, we write for readers. And if the awards come, that's great. And they do make a difference, like the Newbery makes an enormous difference in a career, and even in your backlist. And I certainly never expected to get a Newbery because I thought after thirty years if I'm going to get one I would have got one by now. And then I got one. And then another. So, all I can say about that is it came along at a time in my career when I could appreciate it. I have just received the *Chicago Tribune*'s first young adult award, to be given in October [2002], and I'll be going out on October 26 to accept it. And I think it is significant that it is the *Chicago Tribune* that has established an award for young adults, not the *New York Times*, which is the newspaper of the publishing capital, that has little or no interest in children's books. And to receive the National Humanities medal last spring was very meaningful because no children's writer had ever received one before. That was wonderful, and it is due to Mrs. Laura Bush, who was of course a school librarian before she was a first lady, and she knows who we are. She knows us by name and by work. And so when the National Festival of the Book was held in Washington last September—September 7 and 8, 2001—of the fifty-five authors, almost twenty of us were children's writers and illustrators. And this is the first time we have had a first lady who knows who we are. And, of course, has this mandate for early childhood education. So we must enjoy her while we may. She's doing good work. That award meant a great deal to me because of that.

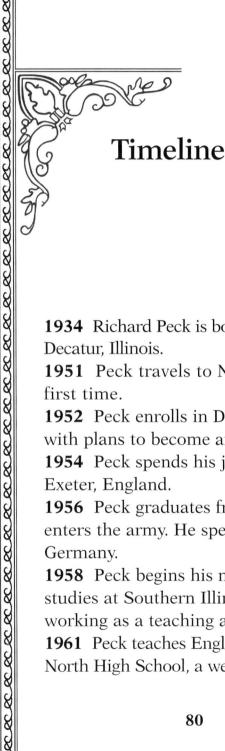

Timeline

1934 Richard Peck is born on April 5 in Decatur, Illinois.

1951 Peck travels to New York for the first time.

1952 Peck enrolls in DePauw University with plans to become an English teacher.

1954 Peck spends his junior year in Exeter, England.

1956 Peck graduates from DePauw and enters the army. He spends two years in Germany.

1958 Peck begins his master's degree studies at Southern Illinois University, working as a teaching assistant in English.

1961 Peck teaches English at Glenbrook North High School, a wealthy Chicago suburb.

1963 Peck works as a textbook editor
in Chicago.
Peck writes and publishes his first book, a
guide to Chicago nightlife, with his friend
Norman Strasma.
1965 Peck moves to New York City to teach
English at Hunter College High School for gifted
girls on Manhattan's Upper East Side.
1971 Peck quits teaching for good to become a
novelist at the age of thirty-seven.
1972 Peck publishes his first novel, *Don't Look
and It Won't Hurt*.
1975 Peck publishes *The Ghost Belonged to Me*,
the first of four novels featuring one of Peck's
best-loved characters, Blossom Culp.
1976 Peck publishes one of his most widely
read and critically acclaimed books, *Are You in
the House Alone?*, one of the first YA novels to
tackle the issue of rape.
1985 Moved by the rise of teen suicides, Peck
publishes the critically acclaimed *Remembering
the Good Times*, which features one of his most
successful elderly characters: Polly Prior.
1990 Peck wins two important awards: the
prestigious Margaret A. Edwards Lifetime
Achievement Award for the entire body of his
work, and the National Council of Teachers of

English/ALAN Award for outstanding contributions to young adult literature.

1991 *Anonymously Yours*, Peck's first auto-biography, is published.

1994 Peck publishes *Love and Death at the Mall: Teaching and Writing for the Literate Young*, a series of autobiographical essays.

1995 Local censorship of his and other novels provoke Peck to write *The Last Safe Place on Earth*.

1998 In *A Long Way from Chicago*, Peck introduces the immensely popular character of Grandma Dowdel. The novel wins a Newbery Honor award.

2001 *A Year Down Yonder*, which chronicles the further adventures of Grandma Dowdel, wins the Newbery Medal.

Fair Weather, Peck's most recent novel, set during the Chicago World's Fair of 1893, is published.

2002 In April, in Washington, D.C., President George W. Bush awards Peck with a National Humanities Medal for creating works that have deepened the nation's understanding of the humanities.

Peck publishes *Invitations to the World: Teaching and Writing for Young People*, an updated version of *Love and Death at the Mall*.

Selected Reviews from *School Library Journal*

Blossom Culp and the Sleep of Death
March 1986

Gr 6 Up—Good news for the Blossom Culp cult! Peck's feisty fourteen-year-old psychic returns for a fourth adventure, set, as always, in Bluff City, sometime around 1914. As in earlier installments of Blossom's antic autobiography . . . *The Sleep of Death* incorporates elements of both the topical and the occult (women's suffrage and the lively spirit of an ancient Egyptian princess, respectively). Complications abound and Blossom, as usual, is culpable. And, yes, her unwilling accomplice is once again the fatuous but good-looking Alexander Armsworth. Also returning are Blossom's chief antagonist, the dreaded Letty

Shambaugh and her coterie of lesser nemeses, the Sunny Thoughts and Busy Fingers Sisterhood. There is no sting in . . . *Death*, but it does seem more contrived in terms of plot and weaker in its setting and use of period than earlier titles in this series. Nevertheless, it is an entertaining and generally well-crafted diversion with moments of inspired humor (the hapless Alexander's fraternity initiation rights) and abundant examples of Peck's gift for turning the humorous phrase ("I was jumpier than turtle parts in a pan"). —Michael Cart, Beverly Hills Public Library, California

The Great Interactive Dream Machine
October 1996

Gr 4–6—The continuing adventures through time, space, and middle school of Josh Lewis and Aaron Zimmer, first introduced in *Lost in Cyberspace* (Dial, 1995). Techno-nerd Aaron has found a formula that allows cyberspace travel through cellular reorganization. Unfortunately, there are bugs in the program that turn the computer into an uncontrollable wish-granting time-travel machine. The boys shun soccer camp, instead attending summer school for history at their exclusive New York City private school. Their study of World War II has surprising results

for their eighty-year-old lonesome neighbor, Miss
Mathers. Humor, fantasy, science fiction, and even
a touch of mystery all cleverly combine to make
this book a guaranteed fun, fast-paced adventure.
—Connie Tyrrell Burns, Mahoney Middle School,
South Portland, Maine

The Last Safe Place on Earth
1995

Gr 6–10—With his picture-perfect family, soph-
omore Todd Tobin lives on Tranquility Lane in
Walden Woods. Elitist, undoubtedly racist, and
subtly sexist, this is a place where people assume
they are safe from harm. Peck paints the surface of
this world as attractive and provides a first-person
narrator with immense appeal and a fine sense of
humor. This calm facade is the backdrop for a truly
terrifying novel. Laurel, who babysits for Todd's
sister Marnie, is a teen who clutches her Christian
self-righteousness as a cloak of safety because of
her dysfunctional family. Her talk of devils, hell,
and evil traumatize the little girl. First the child has
nightmares, and then Todd discovers her trying to
flush her witch costume down the toilet in an eerie
night scene. Other issues, such as censorship in the
community and Todd's geeky friend C. E.'s struggle
to care for himself due to an absent father and an
alcoholic mother cause the family to pull together.

Parental involvement and basic neighborliness are resurrected as solutions. The fundamentalist Christian right is depicted as both frightened and frightening. Walter Dean Myers's *Darnell Rock Reporting* (Delacorte, 1994) is more lighthearted and Avi's *Nothing But the Truth* (Orchard, 1991) more distant from the characters. Through Todd's affection for Laurel, Peck makes readers see that she and her family (if not her church) are not just the opposition, but people entrapped by their narrow-mindedness. The scary and real consequences of letting censors go unchallenged is not denied. As Todd says, "I must have known there is no safe place." —Carol A. Edwards, Minneapolis Public Library, Minnesota

A Long Way from Chicago: A Novel in Stories 1998

Gr 4–8—A rollicking celebration of an eccentric grandmother and childhood memories. Set in the 1930s, the book follows Joe and Mary Alice Dowdel as they make their annual August trek to visit their grandmother who lives in a sleepy Illinois town somewhere between Chicago and St. Louis. A woman with plenty of moxie, she keeps to herself, a difficult task in this small community. However, Grandma Dowdel uses her wit and ability to tell whoppers to get the best of manipulative people or those who put on airs. She takes matters into her own hands to intimidate a father who won't control his unruly sons, and forces the bank to rescind a foreclosure on an elderly woman's house. Whether it's scaring a pretentious newspaper man back to the city or stealing the sheriff's boat and sailing right past him as he drunkenly dances with his buddies at the Rod & Gun Club, she never ceases to amaze her grandchildren with her gall and cunning behavior. Each chapter resembles a concise short story. Peck's conversational style has a true storyteller's wit, humor, and rhythm. Joe, the narrator, is an adult looking back on his childhood memories; in the prologue, readers are reminded that while these tales may seem unbelievable, "all memories are true." Perfect for reading aloud, *A Long Way from Chicago* is a great choice for family sharing. —Shawn Brommer, Southern Tier Library System, Painted Post, New York

Those Summer Girls I Never Met
November 1988

Gr 6–10—Drew and his friend Bates had been putting the finishing touches on their summer fantasies of girls and cars when Drew's single parent mother bursts his balloon, telling him that he and his fourteen-year-old sister Steph (whom he sees as a meddlesome bother) are expected to accept an invitation from their never-before-seen grandmother to be her guests on an all-summer cruise from London to Leningrad. Much to their surprise, Drew and Steph become attached to their grandmother, Connie Carlson, a singer-entertainer who made her mark in the '40s and '50s. Connie brings together Steph and Drew, and they learn about their mother, their grandfather (an alcoholic piano player on board), and about themselves. They also learn the tragic truth about Connie. Drew's first-person narrative is permeated with an appealing mixture of sarcastic and self-deprecating humor similar to Robert Lipsyte's teen heroes. The sub-plots of Steph's shipboard friend's family reuniting in Russia and Drew's attempts to help his grandfather complement the main plot, and Drew's very funny amorous misadventures add a counterbalancing levity to what is basically a serious and believable coming-of-age story. — Jack Forman, Mesa College Library, San Diego, California

List of
Selected Works

Anonymously Yours. Englewood Cliffs, NJ:
   Julian Messner, 1991.
Are You in the House Alone? New York:
   Viking Press, 1976.
Bel-Air Bambi and the Mall Rats. New York:
   Delacorte Press, 1993.
Blossom Culp and the Sleep of Death. New
   York: Delacorte Press, 1986.
Close Enough to Touch. New York: Delacorte
   Press, 1981.
Don't Look and It Won't Hurt. New York:
   Holt, Rinehart & Winston, 1972.
The Dreadful Future of Blossom Culp. New
   York: Delacorte Press, 1983.
Dreamland Lake. New York: Holt, Rinehart
   & Winston, 1973.

Fair Weather. New York: Dial Books, 2001.
Father Figure. New York: Viking Press, 1978.
The Ghost Belonged to Me. New York: Viking
   Press, 1975.
Ghosts I Have Been. New York: Viking Press, 1977.
The Great Interactive Dream Machine. New
   York: Dial Press, 1996.
*Invitations to the World: Teaching and Writing
   for Young People*. New York: Dial Books, 2002.
The Last Safe Place on Earth. New York:
   Delacorte Press, 1995.
A Long Way from Chicago. New York: Dial
   Books, 1998.
Lost in Cyberspace. New York: Dial Books, 1995.
*Love and Death at the Mall: Teaching and
   Writing for the Literate Young*. New York:
   Delacorte Press, 1994.
Princess Ashley. New York: Delacorte Press, 1987.
Remembering the Good Times. New York:
   Delacorte Press, 1985.
Representing Super Doll. New York: Viking
   Press, 1974.
Secrets of the Shopping Mall. New York:
   Delacorte Press, 1979.
Strays Like Us. New York: Dial Books, 1998.
Through a Brief Darkness. New York: Viking
   Press, 1973.

Those Summer Girls I Never Met. New York: Delacorte Press, 1988.

Unfinished Portrait of Jessica. New York: Delacorte Press, 1991.

Voices After Midnight. New York: Delacorte Press, 1989.

A Year Down Yonder. New York: Dial Books, 2000.

List of Selected Awards

Margaret A. Edwards Lifetime
Achievement Award for the entire body
of his work (1990)
National Council of Teachers of
English/ALAN Award for outstanding
contributions to young adult
literature (1990)
National Humanities Medal (2001)
Anne V. Zarrow Award for Young Readers'
Literature (2002)

***A Year Down Yonder* (2000)**
American Library Association Notable
Book (2000)
American Library Association Best Book for
Young Adults (2000)
Booklist Best Book of the Year (2000)

School Library Journal Best Book of the
    Year (2000)
Newbery Medal (2001)

Are You in the House Alone? (1976)
American Library Association Best Book for
    Young Adults (1976)
American Library Association Best of the Best
    Books, Young Adult (1970–1982)
School Library Journal Best Book of the
    Year (1976)
Edgar Allan Poe Mystery Award (1977)

Blossom Culp and the Sleep of Death (1986)
American Library Association Notable Book for
    Children (1986)

Fair Weather (2001)
American Library Association Best Book for
    Young Adults (2001)
School Library Journal Best Book of the
    Year (2001)

Father Figure (1978)
American Library Association Best Book for
    Young Adults (1978)
American Library Association Best of the Best
    Books, Young Adult (1970–1982)

The Last Safe Place on Earth (1995)
American Library Association Best Book for
    Young Adults (1995)

A Long Way from Chicago **(1998)**
Newbery Honor Book (1999)
National Book Award Finalist (1998)
American Library Association Notable
Book (1998)
American Library Association Best Book for
Young Adults (1998)

Princess Ashley **(1987)**
American Library Association Notable
Children's Book (1987)
American Library Association Best Book for
Young Adults (1987)
School Library Journal Best Books of the
Year (1987)

Remembering the Good Times **(1985)**
American Library Association Best Book for
Young Adults (1985)
School Library Journal Best Books of the
Year (1985)

Representing Super Doll **(1974)**
American Library Association Best Books for
Young Adults (1974)

Glossary

adept Skilled, proficient.

anthology A collection of writings by various authors.

antidote Something that relieves, prevents, or counteracts something negative.

banter Good-natured joking around.

Carson McCullers One of the most important American fiction writers of the 20th century, whose novels and short stories often deal with loners and nonconformists.

censor To prohibit or repress something that is considered negative or damaging.

chaplain Church minister who works in schools, prisons, hospitals, or the army.

confidante Someone trusted with intimate secrets.

conformist Someone who obeys and tries to copy established rules or customs.

congregation Group of people coming together, usually for a church service.

defer To delay.

didactic Designed or intended to teach.

dismal Dreadful, gloomy.

eccentric Someone who stands out or separates him/herself from established, usual norms.

fox-trot A type of ballroom dance.

fundamentalist A movement or attitude that demands strict obedience to a rigid, often extreme set of (often religious) beliefs.

irrelevant Unimportant, useless.

irony Mocking or sarcastic type of humor that often plays on double meanings.

maudlin Overly sentimental.

nostalgia A sentimental longing for the past.

octogenarian A person between eighty and eighty-nine years of age.

paradox Someone or something with qualities or ideas that, on the surface, seem to contradict or conflict with each other.

rationing To use something sparingly or in reduced quantities due to a shortage

relevant Important, useful.

rumba A ballroom dance of Cuban origin.

satire A literary work that uses humor, irony, and sarcasm to criticize or ridicule some aspect of human behavior.

spunky Bold, lively in spirit.

squeamish Finicky, delicate, or prissy.

subtle Fine, delicate, or skillful.

tweed A rough woolen fabric.

For More Information

Web Sites

Due to the changing nature of Internet links, the Rosen Publishing Group, Inc., has developed an online list of Web sites related to the subject of this book. This site is updated regularly. Please use this link to access the list:

Http://www.rosenlinks.com/lab/rpec

For Further Reading

Cart, Michael. *From Romance to Realism: 50 Years of Growth and Change in Young Adult Literature*. New York: HarperCollins, 1996.

Gallo, Donald R. *Presenting Richard Peck*. Boston: Twayne Publishers, 1989.

Peck, Richard. *Anonymously Yours*. Englewood Cliffs, NJ: Julian Messner, 1991.

Peck, Richard. *Invitations to the World: Teaching and Writing for Young People*. New York: Dial Books, 2002.

Peck, Richard. *Love and Death at the Mall: Teaching and Writing for the Literate Young*. New York: Delacorte Press, 1994.

Sarkissian, Adele, ed. *Something about the Author Autobiography Series, Vol. 2*. Detroit: Gale Research, 1985, pp. 175–186.

Bibliography

American Library Association. ALA News
Release, "American Library Association
announces award winners; Peck, *Small*
receive Newbery, Caldecott Medals"
January 15, 2001. Retrieved June 25, 2002
(http://www.ala.org/news/v6n9/
awardsfinal.html).

Booklist. Review of *Don't Look and It Won't
Hurt*. February 15, 1973, p. 574.

Cart, Michael. *From Romance to
Realism: 50 Years of Growth and Change
in Young Adult Literature*. New York:
HarperCollins, 1996.

Educational Paperback Association.
Autobiographical sketch written by
Richard Peck for the *Fifth Book of Junior
Authors*, published by H. W. Wilson, 1983.
Retrieved June 24, 2002
(http://www.edupaperback.org/authorbios/
Peck_Richard.html).

Gallo, Donald R. *Presenting Richard Peck*.
Boston: Twayne Publishers, 1989.

Gallo, Donald R., ed. *Speaking for Ourselves: Autobiographical Sketches by Notable Authors of Books for Young Adults.* Urbana, IL: National Council of Teachers of English, 1990.

Heins, Ethel L. Review of *Ghosts I Have Been. The Horn Book Magazine,* February 1978, p. 56

Heins, Paul. Review of *Are You in the House Alone? The Horn Book Magazine,* February 1977, p.60.

Leibold, Cynthia K. Review of *Remembering the Good Times. School Library Journal,* April 1985, p. 99.

Levy, J. W. Review of *Are You in the House Alone? Journal of Reading,* April 1978, p. 655.

Peck, Richard. *Anonymously Yours.* Englewood Cliffs, NJ: Julian Messner, 1991.

Peck, Richard. *Are You in the House Alone?* New York: Viking Press, 1976.

Peck, Richard. "Coming Full Circle: From Lesson Plans to Young Adult Novels." *The Horn Book Magazine,* April 1985, p. 210.

Peck, Richard. *Don't Look and It Won't Hurt.* New York: Henry Holt and Company, 1972.

Peck, Richard. *Father Figure.* New York: Signet Books, 1979.

Peck, Richard. "The Genteel Unshelving of a Book." *School Library Journal,* May 1986, pp. 37–39.

Peck, Richard. *Ghosts I Have Been.* New York: Viking Press, 1977.

Peck, Richard. *The Last Safe Place on Earth.* New York: Delacorte Press, 1995.

Peck, Richard. *A Long Way from Chicago*. New York: Dial Books, 1998.

Peck, Richard. *Love and Death at the Mall: Teaching and Writing for the Literate* Young New York: Delacorte Press, 1994.

Richard Peck. *Remembering the Good Times*. New York: Delacorte Press, 1985.

Peck, Richard. *Representing Super Doll*. New York: Viking Press, 1974.

Peck, Richard. *Secrets of the Shopping Mall*. New York: Delacorte Press, 1979.

Peck, Richard. *Unfinished Portrait of Jessica* New York: Delacorte Press, 1991.

Penguin Putnam Books for Young Readers. "Biography: Richard Peck." Retrieved June 25, 2002 (http://www.penguinputnam.com/ Author/AuthorFrame?0000020017).

Publishers Weekly. Review of *Remembering the Good Times*. May 17, 1985, p. 118.

Richard Peck Home Page. Retrieved August 20, 2002 (http://www.richardpeck.smartwriters.com).

Rochman, Hazel. *Review of Remembering the Good Times. Booklist*, March 1, 1985, p. 945.

Sarkissian, Adele, ed. *Something about the Author Autobiography Series*, Vol. 2. Detroit: Gale Research, 1985, pp. 175–186.

Sutherland, Zena. Review of *Are You in the House Alone? Bulletin for the Center for Children's Books*, March 1977, p. 112.

Tallmania: Richard Peck. Archive from a school visit by the author. Retrieved June 24, 2002 (http://www.tallmania.com/peck.html).

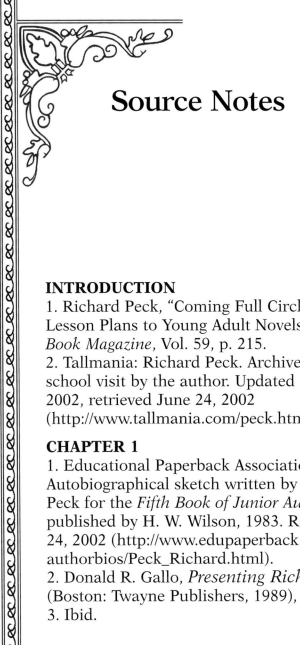

Source Notes

INTRODUCTION
1. Richard Peck, "Coming Full Circle: From Lesson Plans to Young Adult Novels," *The Horn Book Magazine*, Vol. 59, p. 215.
2. Tallmania: Richard Peck. Archive from a school visit by the author. Updated March 10, 2002, retrieved June 24, 2002 (http://www.tallmania.com/peck.html).

CHAPTER 1
1. Educational Paperback Association. Autobiographical sketch written by Richard Peck for the *Fifth Book of Junior Authors*, published by H. W. Wilson, 1983. Retrieved June 24, 2002 (http://www.edupaperback.org/authorbios/Peck_Richard.html).
2. Donald R. Gallo, *Presenting Richard Peck* (Boston: Twayne Publishers, 1989), p. 7.
3. Ibid.

4. Adele Sarkissian, ed., *Something about the Author* Autobiography Series, Vol. 2, (Detroit: Gale Research, 1985), p. 177.
5. Richard Peck, *Anonymously Yours* (Englewood Cliffs, NJ: Julian Messner, 1991), p. 20.
6. Sarkissian, ed., *Something about the Author*, p. 178.
7. Richard Peck. *Representing Super Doll*. (New York: Viking Press, 1974), pp. 12–13.
8. Sarkissian, ed., *Something About the Author*, p. 176.
9. Random House Author/Illustrators: Richard Peck. Retrieved June 24, 2002 (http://www.randomhouse.com/teachers/authors/peck.html).
10. Peck, *Love and Death at the Mall: Teaching and Writing for the Literate Young* (New York, Delacorte Press, 1974), p. 6.

CHAPTER 2
1. Adele Sarkissian, ed., *Something About the Author* Autobiography Series, Vol. 2, (Detroit: Gale Research, 1985), p. 179.
2. Donald R. Gallo, *Presenting Richard Peck* (Boston: Twayne Publishers, 1989), p. 9.
3. Donald R. Gallo., ed. *Speaking for Ourselves: Autobiographical Sketches by Notable Authors of Books for Young Adults*. (Urbana, IL: National Council of Teachers of English, 1990), p. 165.
4. Sarkissian, ed. *Something About the Author*, p. 180.
5. Richard Peck, *Anonymously Yours* (Englewood Cliffs, NJ: Julian Messner, 1991), p. 61.
6. Ibid., p. 62.
7. Ibid.

CHAPTER 3
1. Donald R. Gallo, *Presenting Richard Peck* (Boston: Twayne Publishers, 1989), p. 13.
2. Adele Sarkissian, ed., *Something about the Author* Autobiography Series, Vol. 2 (Detroit: Gale Research, 1985), p. 183.

CHAPTER 4
1. Richard Peck, "Coming Full Circle: From Lesson Plans to Young Adult Novels," *The Horn Book Magazine*, April 1985, p. 210.
2. Richard Peck, *Anonymously Yours* (Englewood Cliffs, NJ: Julian Messner, 1991), p. 85.
3. Ibid., p. 86.
4. Richard Peck. *Love and Death at the Mall: Teaching and Writing for the Literate Young* (New York: Delacorte Press, 1994), p. 112.
5. Ibid.
6. Donald R. Gallo, *Presenting Richard Peck* (Boston: Twayne Publishers, 1989), p. 14.
7. Peck, *Love and Death at the Mall*, p. 55.
8. Ibid., p. 54.
9. Ibid.
10. Richard Peck. "A Teacher's Prayer," *News from Dell Books*. n/d. Reprinted in *Love and Death at the Mall*, p. 62.
11. Richard Peck, *Love and Death at the Mall*.

CHAPTER 5
1. Richard Peck in Viking Press publicity brochure. n/d. Reprinted in Donald R. Gallo, *Presenting Richard Peck* (Boston: Twayne Publishers, 1989), p. 17.
2. Richard Peck, *Don't Look and It Won't*

Hurt (New York: Henry Holt and Company, 1972), pp. 150–151.

3. *Publishers Weekly.* September 25, 1972, p. 60.

4. *Booklist.* February 15, 1973, p. 574.

5. Border's "The Writer's Life" Site. Interview with Richard Peck from 2002. Retrieved August 12, 2002 (http://www.bordersstores.com/ib/200201/ib_features_peck.jsp).

6. Peck, *Love and Death at the Mall: Teaching and Writing for the Literate Young* (New York: Delacorte Press, 1994), p. 65.

7. Ibid.

CHAPTER 6

1. Richard Peck, *Anonymously Yours* (Englewood Cliffs, NJ: Julian Messner, 1991), p. 104.

2. Richard Peck. *Love and Death at the Mall: Teaching and Writing for the Literate Young* (New York: Delacorte Press, 1994), p. 126.

3. Decatur Area Writer's Fair Home Page. 1999 Decatur Writer's Fair Keynote Speaker: Richard Peck. Retrieved June 26, 2002 (http://www.millikin.edu/decaturwritersfair/peck.html).

4. Peck, *Anonymously Yours*, p. 106.

5. Donald R. Gallo, *Presenting Richard Peck* (Boston: Twayne Publishers, 1989), p. 74.

6. Richard Peck, interviewed by Paul Janeczko in *From Writers to Students*, p. 81. Cited in *Presenting Richard Peck*, p. 76.

7. Peck, *Anonymously Yours*, p. 86.

8. Janet Leonberger, Review of *Are You in the House Alone?*, *Young Adult Cooperative Book Review of Massachusetts*, February 1977, p. 89. Cited in

Presenting Richard Peck, p. 76.

9. Zena Sutherland, Review of *Are You in the House Alone?*, *Bulletin of the Center for Children's Books*, March 1977, p. 112.

10. Paul Heins, Review of *Are You in the House Alone?*, *The Horn Book Magazine*, February 1977, p. 60.

11. Gallo, *Presenting Richard Peck*, p. 87.

12. *Publishers Weekly*, July 17, 1978, p. 168.

13. Peck, *Love and Death at the Mall*, p. 96.

14. Gallo, *Presenting Richard Peck*, p. 109.

15. Kay Webb O'Connell, *School Library Journal*, September 1981, p. 140.

16. *Bulletin of the Center for Children's Books*, November 1981, p. 53.

17. Norma Bagnall, *ALAN Review*, Winter 1982, p. 21.

18. Richard Peck, *Love and Death at the Mall*, p. 97.

19. Ibid., pp. 102–103

20. Michael Cart, *From Romance to Realism: 50 Years of Growth and Change in Young Adult Literature* (New York: HarperCollins, 1996), p. 177.

21. Ibid., p. 176.

22. Peck, *Remembering the Good Times*, p. 54.

23. Hazel Rochman, *Booklist*. March 1, 1985, p. 945.

24. Cynthia K.. Leibold, *School Library Journal*, April 1985, p. 99.

25. Kristiana Gregory, *Los Angeles Times Book Review*, August 10, 1986.

26. *Publishers Weekly*, May 17, 1985. p. 118.

CHAPTER 7

1. Richard Peck. *Love and Death at the Mall: Teaching and Writing for the Literate Young*, (New York: Delacorte Press, 1994), p. 109.

2. Ibid.
3. Ibid., p. 110.
4. Donald R. Gallo, *Presenting Richard Peck* (Boston: Twayne Publishers, 1989), p. 67.
5. Ibid., p. 23.
6. Ibid., p. 67.
7. Richard Peck, *Ghosts I Have Been* (New York: Viking, 1977), p. 6.
8. Richard Peck, *Anonymously Yours* (Englewood Cliffs, NJ: Julian Messner, 1991), p. 23.
9. Ibid.
10. Linda Silver, *School Library Journal*, November 1977, p. 63.
11. Richard Peck. "Meet the Author" Children's Book Council Web site (http://www.cbc.books.org).
12. Richard Peck. *A Long Way from Chicago* (New York: Dial,1998), p. 45.
13. The Children's Book Council. *Meet the Author/Illustrator: Richard Peck*. Updated 2001. Retrieved June 25, 2002. (http://www.cbcbooks.org/html/richard_peck.html)
14. Shawn Brommer, *School Library Journal*, October 1998, p. 144.
15. Kitty Flynn, *The Horn Book Magazine*, November/ December 1998, pp. 738–739.
16. The Children's Book Council (http://www.cbcbooks.org/html/richard_peck.html).
17. Peck, *Love and Death at the Mall*, p. 19–20.
18. Ibid., p. 79.
19. Michael Cart, *From Romance to Realism: 50 Years of Growth and Change in Young Adult Literature*, (New York: HarperCollins, 1996), pp. 177–178.

CHAPTER 8

1. Donald R. Gallo, *Presenting Richard Peck* (Boston: Twayne Publishers, 1989), p. 28.
2. Richard Peck, "The Genteel Unshelving of a Book," *School Library Journal*, May 1986, p. 37.
3. Peck, *Love and Death at the Mall*, p. 146.
4. Richard Peck, *The Last Safe Place on Earth* (New York: Delacorte, 1995), p. 173.
5. Random House Author/Illustrators: Richard Peck. Retrieved June 24, 2002 (http://www.randomhouse.com/teachers/authors/peck.html).
6. Tallmania: Richard Peck. Archive from a school visit by the author. Updated March 10, 2002. Retrieved June 24, 2002 (http://www.tallmania.com/peck.html).
7. Ibid.

Index

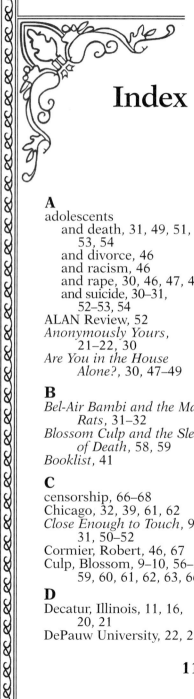

About the Author
Michael A. Sommers is a freelance journalist.

Photo Credits
Cover and p. 2 © Stuart Ramson/AP/Wide World Photos

Series Designer: Tahara Hasan; Editor: Annie Sommers